Sorbets & Granitas

ICY DELIGHTS

SAUCES & COOKIES

ICY DELIGHTS

SAUCES & COOKIES

ICY DELIGHTS

SAUCES & COOKIES

ICY DELIGHTS

SAUCES & COOKIES

ICY DELIGHTS

SAUCES & COOKIES

Sorbets & Granitas

from Duane Park Cafe

Joy Simmen Hamburger & Mimi Shanley Taft

Recipes by John Dudek & Seiji Maeda
of Duane Park Cafe

Illustrations by Joy Simmen Hamburger

TEN SPEED PRESS
Berkeley, California

Ten Speed Press
P.O. Box 7123
Berkeley, CA 94707

A Kirsty Melville book

Distributed in Australia by E.J. Dwyer Pty Ltd; in Canada by Publishers Group West; in New Zealand by Tandem Press; in South Africa by Real Books; in the United Kingdom and Europe by Airlift Books; and in Singapore and Malaysia by Berkeley Books.

Text design by Nancy Austin
Cover design by Nancy Austin and Joy Simmen Hamburger
Printed in Hong Kong

Library of Congress Cataloging-in-Publication Data

Hamburger, Joy
    Sorbets and granitas : icy delights, sauces, and cookies from Duane Park Cafe
    / by Joy Simmen Hamburger and Mimi Shanley Taft.
        p. cm.
    Includes index.
    ISBN 0-89815-902-4
    1. Ice cream, ices, etc. 2. Sauces. I. Taft, Mimi Shanley.
    II. Duane Park Cafe. III. Title.
    TX795.T243 1997
    641.8'63—dc21   96-39423
                                                         CIP

1 2 3 4 5 — 00 99 98 97

ACKNOWLEDGMENTS

We would like to thank chefs John Dudek and Seiji Maeda and general manager Alfred A. Chiodo of Duane Park Cafe for the inspiration, dedicated support, energy, and patience they provided during the completion of this book.

We would also like to thank our friends and family members for their enthusiasm for this project, especially Peter, Zoe, and Max Hamburger, and Lloyd, Daniel, Virginia, and Bennett Taft.

Special thanks to Susan Ginsburg and the staff at Writer's House for all of their efforts in seeing this book to completion.

And final thanks to our editors at Ten Speed Press, Kirsty Melville and Clancy Drake.

CONTENTS

INTRODUCTION

Each summer, faithful patrons gather in lower Manhattan for the Sorbet and Granita Festival at Duane Park Cafe. These icy delights, the creations of pastry chef John Dudek, have become the signature desserts at this popular restaurant, which was founded by chef Seji Maeda.

Originally, sorbets and granitas were delicacies reserved for royal tables. History recounts that Nero had slaves pass buckets filled with snow down from the mountains. The snow was then mixed with fresh fruits and sweet honey, producing an early form of granita. Marco Polo's legendary influence on Italian cooking includes a recipe he brought back from China for a frozen dessert made from ice and fruit. When Italy's Catherine de' Medici married France's King Henry II, she brought with her a prized recipe for sorbetto, which was quickly absorbed into France's culinary tradition. Since then, sorbets and granitas have become so popular in Europe that they are not only available in elegant restaurants, but also at lively sidewalk cafes and street corner vendors.

Sorbets and granitas are variations on the theme of flavored ice. It is most likely that granita is the older of the two. Granitas, a mixture of puréed fruit, water, and sugar, take their name from the Italian word *grana*, which means "grain." Granitas are stirred occasionally while being frozen to create the coarse, grainy texture of ice crystals.

Sorbets, however, must be processed in an ice cream maker to achieve a smooth, creamy texture. Beautiful sorbets and granitas satisfy the urge to end a meal on a sweet note, without the guilt of indulging in a heavier dessert. Because they contain no dairy products, sorbets and granitas are naturally fat free.

Nothing can match the quality of homemade sorbets and granitas made from ripe fresh fruit. At Duane Park Cafe, sorbets are often served grouped in a medley of colors and complementary tastes. Intensely flavored granitas are topped with sauce or creamy zabaglione. Special cookies complete the desserts. In the pages that follow, we offer recipes for the best of these frozen desserts, along with recipes for toppings and cookies to serve alongside. Each of the fifty recipes in this book has been tested and written to make preparation quick and easy. Throughout the book we recommend ways to combine the different components to please the eye and the palate, guaranteeing spectacular results.

Sorbets

Of all the wonderful desserts on the menu at Duane Park Cafe, it is invariably the sorbet plate that is passed around the table by a diner eager to share the pleasures of this icy delight. Delicious jewel-toned sorbets are easy to prepare and simple to serve. A single intensely colored portion of sorbet garnished with a complementary fresh fruit or herb is a visual poem; an inspired grouping of two or three sorbets is a spectacular treat. Here are some facts and tips to guide you in preparing the fat-free, naturally healthful sorbets in this book:

- Choose fruits and herbs at their peak of ripeness. Very ripe fruit is the most fragrant and the most flavorful.

- Several recipes call for poaching fruit with sugar before it is puréed. Warming and softening the fruit in a metal bowl set over a saucepan of steaming water not only sweetens and enhances its flavor, but it also makes the fruit easier to purée.

- Three techniques used in these recipes eliminate the need for simple syrup: poaching the fruit with sugar; blending the fruit and sugar; and allowing the fruit and sugar to stand, or macerate.

- Always make certain that the sugar is completely dissolved before you proceed to the next step in the recipe.

- Use a blender or large-capacity food processor that can hold 5 fluid cups, or purée the fruit in batches.

- A fine-meshed sieve is often required to strain seeds or skins from the purée.

- Use bottled spring water if you prefer its taste to your tap water in recipes that call for water.

- Many of these recipes call for small quantities of alcohol, such as kirsch or Armagnac. These flavorings add sophistication and complexity to sorbets, and contribute to their smooth texture. If you are concerned about the alcohol component, this ingredient may be omitted, although the character of the sorbet will be changed.

- The smooth, creamy texture of sorbet is created by an ice cream maker, which beats air into the mixture as it freezes. A variety of machines are discussed in the equipment section of this book.

- Each recipe makes approximately 1 quart of sorbet, or about 8 servings.

- Just-processed sorbet is too soft to hold a scoop shape. It should be transferred to an airtight container and put in the freezer for a couple of hours to firm the texture and mellow the flavor. Allow a frozen-hard sorbet to sit at room temperature for about 10 minutes before serving to let it reach its optimum texture and flavor.

- Sorbets without alcohol will keep frozen well for 2 weeks. Those stored for more than a few days, especially those with alcohol in their ingredients, should be softened and briskly stirred with a spoon on the day you plan to serve them, then returned to the freezer until 10 minutes before serving.

BLACKBERRY SORBET

2¹/₂ cups boiling water

1 tea bag or 1 tablespoon
  loose English Breakfast
  or Orange Pekoe tea

1¹/₄ cups sugar

3 cups fresh blackberries,
  plus more for garnish

¹/₄ cup freshly squeezed
  lemon juice (about
  1¹/₂ lemons)

2 tablespoons crème de
  cassis liqueur

To make an elegant presentation of this beautiful purple sorbet, reserve a few fresh blackberries to use as a tasty garnish. An exceptional trio of colors and flavors is achieved by grouping Ginger-Peach, Blackberry, and Strawberry sorbets together, accented with a Cinnamon-Walnut Tuile. Frozen blackberries may be substituted for fresh.

Pour the boiling water over the tea and let it steep for 10 minutes. In a medium bowl, toss the 3 cups blackberries with the sugar. Pour the tea, straining it if necessary, into the bowl with the berries. Using the back of a wooden spoon, crush the berries to release their juices. Cover the bowl and let cool slightly.

Pour the berry mixture into a blender or large-capacity food processor. Purée until smooth. Carefully strain through a fine-meshed sieve into a large metal bowl. Stir in the lemon juice and cassis. Refrigerate for 1 hour, then freeze in an ice cream maker according to the manufacturer's instructions.

MAKES ABOUT 1 QUART

BLOOD ORANGE–
ESSENCIA SORBET

2 cups freshly squeezed
blood orange juice
(about 10 to 12
oranges)

3 tablespoons freshly
squeezed lemon juice
(about 1 lemon)

1 1/2 cups sugar

6 tablespoons grated blood
orange zest (about 4 to
6 oranges)

2 cups Essencia wine

1/8 teaspoon salt

*Essencia, a dessert wine
made from Orange
Muscat grapes, is
available from several
California vintners. At
Duane Park Cafe they
favor one from the
Quady vineyard.*

*Blood oranges are available from early
December through February at specialty
stores or through the mail. The bright red
flesh and sweet-tart flavor of blood oranges
make this sorbet an exotic winter treat.
Moro, Ruby, and Sansuinelli are three varieties prized for their exceptionally deep
color.*

Strain the orange juice and lemon juice
through a fine-meshed sieve into a blender
or large-capacity food processor. Add the
sugar and orange zest and purée until the
sugar is dissolved, about 1 minute. Pour into
a medium-sized metal bowl and stir in the
wine and salt. Refrigerate for 1 hour, then
freeze in an ice cream maker according to
the manufacturer's instructions.

MAKES ABOUT 1 QUART

BLUEBERRY-KIRSCH SORBET

6 cups fresh blueberries

1 cup sugar

3/4 cup freshly squeezed lemon juice (about 4 lemons)

1 tablespoon grated lemon zest (about 2 lemons)

1/4 cup kirsch

Kirschwasser, most commonly called kirsch, is a brandy made from small black cherries that grow in the Rhine valley, which winds through Switzerland, France, and Germany.

The sweetness of kirsch enhances the blueberries, creating an intensely flavorful sorbet. It is delicious alone or served with a scoop of vanilla ice cream. Frozen blueberries may be substituted for fresh but will require 15 minutes more cooking time.

Put the blueberries in a large saucepan. Add the sugar, lemon juice, and lemon zest, stirring to combine. Cover the pan with a tightly fitting lid or plastic wrap and cook the berries over low heat until they are tender and begin to release their juices, about 15 minutes.

Remove from the heat and let cool slightly. Transfer to a blender or large-capacity food processor and purée until smooth. Carefully strain into a large metal bowl through a fine-meshed sieve to remove all seeds. Stir in the kirsch. Refrigerate for 1 hour, then freeze in an ice cream maker according to the manufacturer's instructions.

MAKES ABOUT 1 QUART

CHOCOLATE-RUM SORBET

2 cups hot freshly
brewed coffee

3 ounces bittersweet
chocolate, finely
chopped

1 cup unsweetened cocoa
powder

2/3 cup sugar

1/4 cup dark rum, such
as Myers's

2 teaspoons grated orange
zest (about 1 orange)

1 tablespoon pure
vanilla extract

Myers's Rum is a dark, rich rum that is naturally and slowly fermented. An amber rum, such as Mount Gay, may be substituted in this recipe.

Chocolate lovers rejoice! Top a piece of pound cake with this rich sorbet or savor it alone as a satisfying low-fat treat. For a dramatic presentation, serve this deeply colored sorbet with the vivid and intensely flavored Pomegranate and Blood Orange sorbets, with a Hazelnut Zebra Cookie alongside.

In a medium bowl, whisk together the hot coffee and chocolate. Set aside.

Sift together the cocoa and sugar and place in a blender or large-capacity food processor. With the machine running, add the coffee mixture in a steady stream. Blend until smooth. Stir in the rum, orange zest, and vanilla. Pour into a metal bowl, refrigerate for 1 hour, then freeze in an ice cream maker according to the manufacturer's instructions.

MAKES ABOUT 1 QUART

COCONUT SORBET

1 coconut

3 cups warm milk

1/4 cup sugar

1 tablespoon pure vanilla
extract

2 tablespoons kirsch

1 tablespoon freshly
squeezed lemon juice
(about 1/2 lemon)

1/8 teaspoon salt

*Choose heavy whole
coconuts that are
full of liquid.*

*This sorbet has the creamy consistency of
ice cream. While not as low in fat as most,
it is a very popular sorbet flavor. For a
classic combination of flavors, serve with
Chocolate-Rum Sorbet.*

Preheat the oven to 325°.

Puncture the three eyes of the coconut
with a corkscrew or a sharp knife point.
Drain all the liquid into a glass and set aside.

Place the coconut on a baking sheet
and bake for 20 minutes, or until the shell
cracks. Remove the coconut from the oven
and wrap in a dish towel. Place it on a
cutting board and hit it with a hammer to
crack the shell into several pieces. With the
point of a knife, pry the white flesh from the
coconut shell. Use a vegetable peeler to
remove the brown skin from the white meat.
Cut the coconut meat into small chunks and
place in a blender or large-capacity food
processor. Add the reserved coconut juice
and 1 cup of the warm milk. Purée until
smooth. Add the remaining warm milk as
necessary to bring the total to 5 cups of
coconut purée. Let steep for 45 minutes.

Strain the coconut purée through a fine-meshed sieve into a large metal bowl, pressing on the solids with the back of a large spoon to extract all the liquid. Discard the solids.

Return the coconut purée to the blender or food processor and add the sugar, vanilla extract, kirsch, lemon juice, and salt. Purée until the sugar dissolves, about 1 minute. Return to the bowl and refrigerate for 1 hour, then freeze in an ice cream maker according to the manufacturer's instructions.

MAKES ABOUT 1 QUART

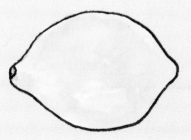

CONCORD GRAPE SORBET

2 pounds Concord grapes

2 tablespoons sugar

1/2 cup water

2 teaspoons light corn syrup

1 tablespoon pear brandy

The essence of pure grape flavor is celebrated in this simple sorbet. Look for fresh Concord grapes in late summer and early fall. For an exceptional combination of hues and flavors, serve this sorbet with Orange-Armagnac and Plum sorbets.

Concord grapes are grown mainly on the East Coast and distributed throughout much of the country. In western states, look for the dark purple California Niabell, also available in late summer and early fall.

Combine the grapes, sugar, water, and corn syrup in a small saucepan. Cover and bring to a boil over medium heat. Remove from the heat, cover, and let sit until cool, about 1 hour.

Strain the mixture through a fine-meshed sieve over a large metal bowl, pressing the fruit with the back of a large spoon to extract as much liquid as possible. Discard the seeds and pulp. Stir the pear brandy into the pear mixture. Refrigerate for 1 hour, then freeze in an ice cream maker according to the manufacturer's instructions.

MAKES ABOUT 1 QUART

Pear brandy, or Poire William, is a clear pear eau de vie from Switzerland. Less expensive brands of pear eau de vie are produced in California.

LEMONGRASS SORBET

1/3 cup thinly sliced lemongrass (about 7 stalks)

2 cups sugar

2 cups dry white wine

1 cup water

1 cup freshly squeezed
lemon juice (about
6 lemons)

2 tablespoons grated lemon
zest (about 3 lemons)

*Fresh lemongrass is
becoming widely avail-
able and can be found
in grocery stores,
gourmet shops, and
ethnic markets. It is
also available by mail.
Please refer to the
Ingredient Sources in
the back of this book
for further information.*

*Fresh lemon juice, lemon zest, and lemon-
grass combine to create a complex and
deliciously flavorful sorbet. It pairs beauti-
fully with Blackberry, Blueberry-Kirsch,
Strawberry-Champagne or Raspberry-Ginger-
Lemonade sorbets as well as with Concord
Grape and Pomegranate sorbets.*

In a small, heavy saucepan, combine the
lemongrass, sugar, and white wine. Cover
and bring to a boil. Remove from heat,
cover, and let sit until cool, about 1 hour.

When cool, strain the mixture through
a fine-meshed sieve into a large metal bowl.
Add the water, lemon juice, and lemon zest.
Refrigerate for 1 hour, then freeze in an
ice cream maker according to the manufacturer's instructions.

MAKES ABOUT 1 QUART

MANGO-LIME SORBET

5 ripe mangoes

1 cup sugar

1/2 teaspoon grated lime zest (about 1 lime)

4 tablespoons freshly squeezed lime juice (about 3 limes)

The peak season for mangoes is from May through September, although imported fruit is often available during the rest of the year. The skin of a mango should be smooth, unbruised, and firm. Gently press the fruit with your thumb; a ripe mango will give slightly.

This sorbet balances the exotic sweetness of mangoes with the refreshing flavor of lime juice. Consider grouping Mango-Lime Sorbet with Coconut and Papaya sorbets for a tropical sorbet sampler.

Slice off the tops and bottoms of the mangoes. Use a vegetable peeler to remove the thin, tough skin. Cut the flesh away from the large flat seed and place the flesh in a blender or large-capacity food processor. Purée until smooth.

Pour the purée into a large metal bowl and whisk in the sugar, zest, and lime juice. Let sit for about 15 minutes, stirring occasionally, until the sugar dissolves. Refrigerate for 1 hour, then freeze in an ice cream maker according to the manufacturer's instructions.

MAKES ABOUT 1 QUART

ORANGE-ARMAGNAC SORBET

3/4 cup sugar

1 tablespoon grated
orange zest (about
2 oranges)

4 cups of freshly squeezed
tangelo juice (about 4
pounds, or 12 oranges)

3 tablespoons freshly
squeezed lemon juice
(about 1 lemon)

1/8 teaspoon salt

1/4 cup Armagnac

Armagnac is an excellent brandy produced from white grapes in southeastern Bordeaux, in France. A cognac or high-quality brandy may be substituted for Armagnac.

Citrus fruits are winter's gift. Try variations of this recipe using fresh, tangy tangelos, honeybell oranges, or even clementines. In early winter, pair this with Pomegranate Sorbet.

Put the sugar and orange zest in a blender or large-capacity food processor and pulse to combine. Strain the orange juice and lemon juice through a fine-meshed sieve and add to the sugar and zest mixture. Blend until the sugar dissolves, about 1 minute.

Transfer the orange mixture to a large metal bowl and stir in the salt and Armagnac. Refrigerate for 1 hour, then freeze in an ice cream maker according to the manufacturer's instructions.

MAKES ABOUT 1 QUART

GINGER-PEACH SORBET

2 pounds ripe fresh peaches, peeled and thinly sliced (about 6 peaches)

3/4 cup sugar

1 tablespoon freshly squeezed lemon juice (about 1/2 lemon)

1 cup freshly squeezed orange juice (about 3 oranges)

One 2-inch piece gingerroot

2 teaspoons grated lemon zest (about 1 lemon)

Fresh ginger adds even more life to this seasonal favorite. If you crave the unique flavor of this sorbet when fresh peaches are not in season, frozen peaches may be substituted. They will require about 15 minutes more cooking time. An exceptional medley of cool tints and tastes is achieved when this sorbet is served with Strawberry-Champagne and Blackberry sorbets, with a Pecan Sandie or two nestled close by.

Fill a large saucepan one-third full of water. Bring to a gentle boil, then reduce heat to a simmer.

In a large metal bowl, toss the peaches with the sugar, lemon juice, and orange juice. Set the bowl on top of the saucepan. Heat the peaches, stirring periodically, until the sugar dissolves and the peaches have softened, about 15 to 20 minutes.

Meanwhile, peel the gingerroot, cut it into small pieces, and process in a blender or large-capacity food processor until finely shredded. Transfer to the center of a piece of cheesecloth or muslin, or a smooth-textured kitchen towel. Gather up the ends and twist the cloth over a small bowl to squeeze out 1 tablespoon of ginger juice. Discard the ginger and set the juice aside.

Allow the peaches to cool slightly, then purée in the blender or food processor until smooth. Return the peach purée to the bowl and stir in the lemon zest and ginger juice. Refrigerate for 1 hour, then freeze in an ice cream maker according to the manufacturer's instructions.

MAKES ABOUT 1 QUART

PAPAYA SORBET

1¹/₂ cups freshly squeezed orange juice (about 5 oranges)

1 cup sugar

5 papayas halved, seeded, and fruit scooped out (about 3 cups flesh)

¹/₃ cup freshly squeezed lime juice (about 4 limes)

1 tablespoon kirsch

¹/₈ teaspoon salt

A ripe papaya has a vivid yellow-orange skin that gives slightly to thumb pressure and emits a sweet aroma. The shiny, peppery flavored gray seeds are edible and make a great addition to salad dressing.

Sweet papayas, sparked with lime juice, make a vibrant, flavorful sorbet. History's earliest known reference to papayas was made by Christopher Columbus. In his journal he noted that the natives of the West Indies were "very strong and live largely on a tree melon called 'the fruit of the angels.'"

In a medium bowl, combine the orange juice and sugar, and stir until the sugar dissolves. Combine the papayas and lime juice in a blender or large-capacity food processor and purée until smooth. With the machine running, add the orange juice mixture in a steady stream. Transfer the purée to a large metal bowl and stir in the kirsch and salt. Refrigerate for 1 hour, then freeze in an ice cream maker according to the manufacturer's instructions.

MAKES ABOUT 1 QUART

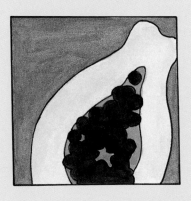

PLUM SORBET

2 pounds purple plums, pitted and quartered

1 cup freshly squeezed orange juice (about 3 oranges)

1 cup sugar

1 teaspoon grated orange zest (about 1 orange)

1 tablespoon Grand Marnier

1/8 teaspoon salt

Even less than perfectly ripe plums are fine for this sorbet. The plums will soften when poached in the sweetened orange juice. Grand Marnier is an orange-flavored liqueur of excellent quality that is produced exclusively in France. Although plain brandy may be substituted, the delicate orange flavor would be missed.

Plums are enjoyed around the world, growing on every continent except Antarctica. They have been cultivated for centuries and were among the foods eaten at the first Thanksgiving feast. Celebrate summer's bounty of fresh fruits by pairing this sorbet with Strawberry-Champagne, Blueberry-Kirsch, or Blackberry sorbets.

Fill a large saucepan one third full of water. Bring to a gentle boil, then reduce heat to a simmer.

In a large metal bowl, toss the plums with the orange juice and sugar. Set the bowl on top of the saucepan of simmering water. Heat the plums, stirring occasionally, until the sugar dissolves and the plums have softened, about 20 minutes. Set aside to cool slightly.

Purée the plums in a blender or large-capacity food processor until smooth. Strain the purée through a fine-meshed sieve into the metal bowl and stir in the orange zest, Grand Marnier, and salt. Refrigerate for 1 hour, then freeze in an ice cream maker according to the manufacturer's instructions.

MAKES ABOUT 1 QUART

POMEGRANATE SORBET

10 to 12 pomegranates

1¼ cups sugar

¼ cup plus 2 tablespoons freshly squeezed lime juice (about 3 limes)

2 teaspoons grated lime zest (about 1 lime)

Pomegranates have a short season. Look for them in October and November. They will keep well for up to two months in the refrigerator.

The exotic pomegranate was cultivated by King Solomon. It is prized for the hundreds of translucent jewel-red seeds hidden beneath its leathery exterior. This uncomplicated sorbet celebrates the pomegranate's sweet-tart flavor and brilliant color.

Cut the pomegranates in half and scrape the seeds into a blender or food mill. Reserve 1 or 2 teaspoonfuls of the seeds to use as garnish. Pulverize the remaining seeds and strain the juice through a fine-meshed sieve into a large metal bowl, pressing with the back of a large spoon on the seeds to extract all of the juice. You will need 3 cups of juice. Add the sugar, lime juice, and lime zest. Let sit, stirring occasionally, until the sugar dissolves, about 15 minutes. Refrigerate for 1 hour, then freeze in an ice cream maker according to the manufacturer's instructions. Serve garnished with the reserved pomegranate seeds.

MAKES ABOUT 1 QUART

RASPBERRY-GINGER
LEMONADE SORBET

4 or 5 lemons

2 cups sugar

2 cups water

2 cups fresh raspberries

One 4-inch piece of ginger-root, peeled and cut into 1/4-inch slices

Three great flavors combine to create this complex, vibrant sorbet. Create a beautiful grouping of hues and flavors by presenting this sorbet with Plum and Concord Grape sorbets, accompanied with an Almond Shortbread Cookie. When fresh raspberries are not in season, frozen raspberries may be substituted. They will require about 15 minutes more steeping time.

Juice the lemons to yield 3/4 cup of juice and set aside; reserve the rinds. Combine the sugar and water in a small saucepan and bring to a boil. Remove from heat and add the raspberries, ginger, and reserved lemon rinds. Stir and let steep for 15 minutes.

Remove the ginger and lemon rinds, squeezing the rinds to extract all the liquid. Purée the raspberry mixture in a blender or large-capacity food processor until smooth. Strain the raspberry purée through a fine-meshed sieve into a large bowl and stir in the lemon juice. Refrigerate for 1 hour, then freeze in an ice cream maker according to the manufacturer's instructions.

MAKES ABOUT 1 QUART

STRAWBERRY-CHAMPAGNE SORBET

4 cups strawberries, hulled and thinly sliced

$^2/_3$ cup sugar

$1^2/_3$ cups dry champagne

2 tablespoons grated lemon zest (about 2 lemons)

6 tablespoons freshly squeezed lemon juice (about 2 lemons)

A split of champagne (350 mL), provides the perfect amount for this recipe. Duane Park Cafe uses a domestic sparkling wine such as Roederer Estate or Domaine Carneros, both excellent California wines propagated from French grapes.

A delicate, sophisticated sorbet. It is also delicious when grouped with the cool, crisp flavors of Blackberry and Plum sorbets.

Fill a large saucepan one-third full with water. Bring to a gentle boil, then reduce heat to a simmer.

In a large metal bowl, toss the strawberries with the sugar. Set the bowl on top of the saucepan of simmering water. Heat the strawberries until the sugar dissolves and the berries have softened, about 10 minutes. Set aside to cool slightly.

Purée the strawberries in a blender or large-capacity food processor until smooth. Return the strawberry purée to the bowl and stir in the champagne, lemon zest, and lemon juice. Refrigerate for 1 hour, then freeze in an ice cream maker according to the manufacturer's instructions.

MAKES ABOUT 1 QUART

Granitas

The basic technique of making granita has not changed very much from the days when Nero's slaves mixed fruits and honey into Alpine snow for presentation at the royal table. Granitas require no modern equipment, save a refrigerator freezer. With just a fork in hand and the recipes in this section, you can create icy concoctions to delight friends and family. At Duane Park Cafe, chef John Dudek tops granita with a dollop of sauce and pairs it with special cookies. His suggestions for such combinations are given in the introductions to the recipes. Here are some additional facts and tips to help you create perfect granita:

- Choose fruits and herbs at their peak of ripeness. Very ripe fruit is the most fragrant and the most flavorful.
- Poaching the fruit with sugar before it is puréed not only sweetens and enhances its flavor, but it also makes the fruit easier to purée.
- Three techniques used in these recipes eliminate the need for a simple syrup: poaching the fruit with sugar; blending the fruit and sugar; and allowing the fruit and sugar to stand, or macerate.
- Always make certain that the sugar is completely dissolved before you proceed to the next step in the recipe.
- Use a blender or large-capacity food processor that can hold up to 5 fluid cups, or purée the fruit in batches.

- A fine-meshed sieve is often required to strain seeds or skins from the purée.

- Use bottled spring water if you prefer its taste to your tap water in recipes that call for water.

- Many of these recipes call for small quantities of alcohol, such as kirsch or Armagnac. These flavorings add sophistication and complexity to granita. If you are concerned about the alcohol component this ingredient may be omitted, although the character of the granita will be changed.

- Choose a nonreactive metal baking pan about 15 by 9 by 2 inches to freeze granita. Larger or smaller pan sizes are fine as long as they fit in your freezer and you adjust the freezing time accordingly.

- A fork is the best tool to use to rake the granita, breaking up large ice crystals in the granita as it freezes.

- Each recipe makes approximately 2 quarts of granita, or about 8 servings.

- Granitas will retain their full flavor for about 2 weeks if stored in an airtight container. Rake through granita before serving to ensure uniformed flavor and consistency.

- To create a sparkling drink, fill a tall glass with granita and top it with seltzer or sparkling water.

GREEN APPLE GRANITA

1/2 cup freshly squeezed lemon juice (about 3 lemons)

1 cup water

6 Granny Smith apples

1/2 cup sugar

2 teaspoons grated lemon zest (about 1 lemon)

Since Granny Smith apples are both imported and domestic, they are available year-round.

Offer this light granita after a hearty autumn meal. Pair it with Burnt Sugar and Calvados Zabaglione and Pistachio Biscotti for an impressive dessert.

Chill a rectangular metal baking pan (about 15 by 9 by 2 inches) in the freezer.

In a large bowl, combine the lemon juice and water. Peel, core, and thinly slice the apples, adding them to the bowl and tossing them as you go. Transfer to a blender or large-capacity food processor and add the sugar. Purée until smooth, about 2 minutes. Strain through a fine-meshed sieve into a bowl, pressing the pulp with the back of a spoon to extract any liquid. Stir in the lemon zest.

Pour the apple mixture into the chilled baking pan and freeze until ice crystals form around the sides and bottom of the pan, about 30 minutes. Carefully rake the mixture with a fork to loosen the ice crystals. Gently stir with the fork until the frozen and unfrozen elements are evenly combined. Do not break the crystals too finely, but do break up any large clumps that may have formed near the edges. Return to the freezer. Repeat this process every 20 minutes until the granita is the uniform consistency of soft crushed ice. This entire process will take about 2 hours in most freezers.

Serve immediately, or store in an airtight container in the freezer.

MAKES ABOUT 2 QUARTS

CHERRY GRANITA

2 pounds sweet cherries, halved and pitted

1/4 cup sugar

2 teaspoons grated lemon zest (about 1 lemon)

3 tablespoons kirsch

1/8 teaspoon salt

3 tablespoons freshly squeezed lemon juice (about 1 lemon)

1/3 cup freshly squeezed orange juice, strained (about 1 orange)

Sweet dark cherries such as Bing, Lambert, and Tarrian are excellent choices for this granita. Frozen cherries may be substituted when fresh are unavailable.

Fresh cherries create a beautiful, sweet granita. Top with Apricot-Tea Infusion and serve a Hazelnut Zebra Cookie on the side.

Chill a rectangular metal baking pan (about 15 by 9 by 2 inches) in the freezer.

Toss the cherries with the sugar, lemon zest, kirsch, and salt. Cover and let sit until the sugar dissolves, about 15 minutes. Transfer to a blender or large-capacity food processor and purée until smooth. Strain through a fine-meshed sieve into a bowl, pressing the fruit with the back of a spoon to extract as much liquid as possible. Stir in the lemon and orange juices.

Pour the mixture into the chilled baking pan and freeze until ice crystals form around the sides and bottom of the pan, about 30 minutes. Rake the mixture with a fork to loosen the ice crystals. Gently stir with the fork until the frozen and unfrozen elements are evenly combined. Do not break the crystals too finely, but do break up any large clumps that may have formed near the edges. Return to the freezer. Repeat this process every 20 minutes until the granita has the consistency of soft crushed ice. This will take about 2 hours in most freezers. Serve immediately, or store in an airtight container in the freezer.

MAKES ABOUT 2 QUARTS

CHOCOLATE GRANITA

4 ounces bittersweet
  chocolate

1/4 cup unsweetened cocoa
  powder

1 cup hot freshly brewed
  coffee

3 cups warm water

1 tablespoon pure vanilla
  extract

1 tablespoon sugar

3 tablespoons grated
  orange zest (about
  2 oranges)

1/8 teaspoon salt

*Serve this satisfyingly rich tasting granita
with Strawberry Zabaglione and Cardamom-
Orange Cookies.*

Chill a rectangular metal baking pan (about
15 by 9 by 2 inches) in the freezer. Fill a
large saucepan one-third full of water. Bring
to a gentle boil, then reduce heat to a simmer.

Melt the chocolate in a large metal bowl
set over the saucepan of simmering water.
Whisk in the cocoa, then the coffee. Remove
from heat and whisk in the water, vanilla,
sugar, orange zest, and salt. Cover and refrigerate for 1 hour.

Pour the chocolate mixture into the
chilled baking pan and freeze until ice crystals form around the sides and bottom of the
pan, about 30 minutes. Carefully rake the
mixture with a fork to loosen the ice crystals. Gently stir with the fork until the
frozen and unfrozen elements are evenly
combined. Do not break the crystals too
finely, but do break up any large clumps
that may have formed near the edges. Return
to the freezer. Repeat this process every 20
minutes until the granita is the uniform consistency of soft crushed ice. This will take
about 2 hours in most freezers.

Serve immediately, or store in an airtight
container in the freezer.

MAKES ABOUT 2 QUARTS

CRANBERRY GRANITA

3 1/3 cups freshly squeezed orange juice (about 10 oranges)

3 tablespoons freshly squeezed lemon juice (about 1 lemon)

1/2 cup sugar

One 1/2-inch-thick slice gingerroot, peeled and cut in thirds

Two 1/8-inch-thick rounds of jalapeño chile, seeds removed

2 cups fresh cranberries, finely chopped (about 8 ounces)

3 tablespoons grated orange zest (about 2 oranges)

1/8 teaspoon salt

1/4 cup Grand Marnier

Hints of ginger and jalapeño add depth to the classic flavors of cranberry and orange. For a remarkable winter treat, serve this granita topped with Lemon-Chardonnay Zabaglione and Cardamom-Orange Cookies. Frozen cranberries may be substituted for fresh, but will require 15 minutes of additional steeping time.

Chill a rectangular metal baking pan (about 15 by 9 by 2 inches) in the freezer.

Strain the orange and lemon juices through a fine-meshed sieve into a medium saucepan. Add the sugar and bring to a boil. Remove from heat and add the ginger and jalapeño. Stir and let steep for 15 minutes.

Remove the ginger and jalapeño. Add the cranberries and bring to a boil, then simmer until tender, about 15 minutes. Remove from heat and stir in the orange zest, salt, and Grand Marnier. Pour cranberry mixture into a metal bowl, cover, and refrigerate for 1 hour.

Pour the cranberry mixture into the chilled baking pan and freeze until ice crystals form around the sides and bottom of the pan, about 30 minutes. Carefully rake the mixture with a fork to loosen the ice crystals. Gently stir with the fork until the frozen and unfrozen elements are evenly

combined. Do not break the crystals too finely, but do break up any large clumps that may have formed near the edges. Return to the freezer and repeat this process every 20 minutes until the granita is the uniform consistency of soft crushed ice. This entire process will take about 2 hours in most freezers.

Serve immediately, or store in an air-tight container in the freezer.

MAKES ABOUT 2 QUARTS

ESPRESSO GRANITA

1/3 cup sugar

2 1/2 cups hot freshly
  brewed espresso coffee

1/4 cup Tia Maria liqueur

1/4 cup Kahlúa liqueur

1 1/2 cups water

2 tablespoons grated
  lemon zest (about
  3 lemons)

*The espresso coffee for
this recipe can be made
in any coffeepot, using
regular or decaffeinated
Italian espresso ground
for your coffeemaker.*

*This is the most popular granita flavor in
Italy. Serve topped with a generous dollop of
Strawberry Zabaglione and with Chocolate–
Macadamia Nut Biscotti on the side for a
truly delicious dessert.*

Chill a rectangular metal baking pan (about
15 by 9 by 2 inches) in the freezer.

Place the sugar in a large metal bowl
and pour the hot coffee over it. Stir until the
sugar dissolves. Allow to cool slightly. Add
the Tia Maria, Kahlúa, water, and lemon
zest. Cover and refrigerate for 1 hour.

Pour the espresso mixture into the
chilled baking pan and freeze until ice crystals form around the sides and bottom of the
pan, about 30 minutes. Carefully rake the
mixture with a fork to loosen the ice crystals.
Gently stir with the fork until the frozen and
unfrozen elements are evenly combined. Do
not break the crystals too finely, but do
break up any large clumps that may have
formed near the edges. Return to the freezer.
Repeat this process every 20 minutes, until
the granita is the uniform consistency of soft
crushed ice. This entire process will take
about 2 hours in most freezers.

Serve immediately, or store in an airtight container in the freezer.

MAKES ABOUT 2 QUARTS

PINK GRAPEFRUIT GRANITA

4 cups freshly squeezed
  pink grapefruit juice
  (about 6 grapefruits)
6 tablespoons sugar
1/8 teaspoon salt

Fresh grapefruits are available most of the year. Those grown in Arizona and California are in the markets from January through August. The Florida and Texas varieties arrive in mid-October and last through June.

Enjoy the fresh flavor and delicate color of this granita alone or topped with Black Currant–Cabernet Sauce and served with Almond Shortbread Cookies.

Chill a rectangular metal baking pan (about 15 by 9 by 2 inches) in the freezer.

Strain the grapefruit juice through a fine-meshed sieve into a medium bowl. Add the sugar and salt, whisking until the sugar dissolves.

Pour the grapefruit mixture into the chilled baking pan. Freeze until ice crystals form around the sides and bottom of the pan, about 30 minutes. Carefully rake the mixture with a fork to loosen the ice crystals. Gently stir with the fork until the frozen and unfrozen elements are evenly combined. Do not break the crystals too finely, but do break up any large clumps that may have formed near the edges. Return to the freezer. Repeat this process every 20 minutes until the granita is the uniform consistency of soft crushed ice. This entire process will take about 2 hours in most freezers.

Serve immediately, or store in an airtight container in the freezer.

MAKES ABOUT 2 QUARTS

HONEYDEW GRANITA

4 pounds honeydew
melon, seeded, rind
removed, and cut into
small chunks (about
7 cups of fruit)

3 tablespoons freshly
squeezed lime juice
(about 2 limes)

1/4 cup sugar

1 teaspoon grated lime zest
(about 1 lime)

This lovely pale green granita is heaven on a hot summer day, especially when paired with Beaumes de Venise Zabaglione and Blueberry-Almond Biscotti.

Chill a rectangular metal baking pan (about 15 by 9 by 2 inches) in the freezer.

In a blender or large-capacity food processor, combine the melon, lime juice, and sugar. Purée for 1 minute, or until the mixture is smooth and the sugar has completely dissolved. Pour the purée into a bowl and stir in the lime zest.

Pour the honeydew mixture into the chilled baking pan and freeze until ice crystals form around the sides and bottom of the pan, about 30 minutes. Carefully rake the mixture with a fork to loosen the ice crystals. Gently stir with the fork until the frozen and unfrozen elements are evenly combined. Do not break the crystals too finely, but do break up any large clumps that may have formed near the edges. Return to the freezer. Repeat this process every 20 minutes until the granita is the uniform consistency of soft crushed ice. This entire process will take about 2 hours in most freezers.

Serve immediately, or store in an airtight container in the freezer.

MAKES ABOUT 2 QUARTS

LEMON GRANITA

1 cup freshly squeezed
lemon juice (about
6 lemons)

2 cups water

¾ cup sugar

2 tablespoons grated lemon
zest (about 3 lemons)

*The white pith beneath
the zest, or yellow
portion of a lemon's
rind, is harshly bitter.
Be careful not to
include it with the zest.*

Chilled margarita glasses are a perfect choice for serving this granita. Top with Raspberry-Champagne Zabaglione and serve Cardamom-Orange Cookies alongside for a refreshing treat.

Chill a rectangular metal baking pan (about 15 by 9 by 2 inches) in the freezer.

In a blender or large-capacity food processor, combine the lemon juice, water, sugar, and lemon zest. Purée until the sugar dissolves, about 1 minute.

Pour the lemon mixture into the chilled baking pan and freeze until ice crystals form around the sides and bottom of the pan, about 30 minutes. Carefully rake the mixture with a fork to loosen the ice crystals. Gently stir with the fork until the frozen and unfrozen elements are evenly combined. Do not break the crystals too finely, but do break up any large clumps that may have formed near the edges. Return to the freezer. Repeat this process every 20 minutes until the granita is the uniform consistency of soft crushed ice. This entire process will take about 2 hours in most freezers.

Serve immediately, or store in an air-tight container in the freezer.

MAKES ABOUT 2 QUARTS

NECTARINE GRANITA

2 pounds (about 6) ripe nectarines, peeled, pitted, and cut into sections

$^1/_2$ cup freshly squeezed lemon juice (about 3 lemons)

$^1/_2$ cup sugar

$^1/_2$ teaspoon ground nutmeg

1 teaspoon grated lemon zest (about 1 lemon)

1 teaspoon pure vanilla extract

Accent this colorful, tangy granita with a dollop of Lemon-Chardonnay Zabaglione and a Pecan Sandie.

Chill a rectangular metal baking pan (about 15 by 9 by 2 inches) in the freezer.

Fill a large saucepan one-third full with water. Bring to a gentle boil, then reduce heat to a simmer.

In a large metal bowl, combine the nectarines, lemon juice, sugar and nutmeg. Set the bowl on top of the saucepan. Cover the bowl with a tightly fitting lid or plastic wrap. Heat the mixture until the sugar dissolves and the fruit has begun to soften, about 15 minutes. Set aside to cool slightly. Purée the mixture in a blender or large-capacity food processor until smooth. Stir in the lemon zest and vanilla. Return to the metal bowl, cover, and refrigerate for 1 hour.

Pour the nectarine mixture into the chilled baking pan and freeze until ice crystals form around the sides and bottom of the pan, about 30 minutes. Carefully rake the mixture with a fork to loosen the ice crystals. Gently stir with the fork until the frozen and unfrozen elements are evenly combined. Do not break the crystals too finely, but do break up any large clumps that may have formed near the edges. Return to the freezer. Repeat this process every 20 minutes until the granita is the uniform consistency of soft crushed ice. This entire process will take about 2 hours in most freezers.

Serve immediately, or store in an airtight container in the freezer.

MAKES ABOUT 2 QUARTS

LIME-MINT GRANITA

Cool and refreshing! Especially when topped with Blackberry Zabaglione and served with Cinnamon-Walnut Tuiles.

2 cups loosely packed fresh mint leaves

1 cup sugar

3 cups water

1 cup freshly squeezed lime juice (about 8 to 10 limes)

1 tablespoon grated lime zest (about 2 limes)

Chill a rectangular metal baking pan (about 15 by 9 by 2 inches) in the freezer.

Put the mint leaves in a blender or large-capacity food processor. Add the sugar, water, and lime juice and purée for 1 minute, or until the sugar has completely dissolved. Strain through a fine-meshed sieve into a large bowl. Stir in the lime zest.

Pour the lime mixture into the chilled baking pan and freeze until ice crystals form around the sides and bottom of the pan, about 30 minutes. Carefully rake the mixture with a fork to loosen the ice crystals. Gently stir with the fork until the frozen and unfrozen elements are evenly combined. Do not break the crystals too finely, but do break up any large clumps that may have formed near the edges. Return to the freezer and repeat this process every 20 minutes until the granita is the uniform consistency of soft crushed ice. This entire process will take about 2 hours in most freezers.

Serve immediately, or store in an air-tight container in the freezer.

MAKES ABOUT 2 QUARTS

TANGERINE GRANITA

5 cups freshly squeezed
tangerine juice (about
12 tangerines)

3 teaspoons grated
tangerine zest (about
2 tangerines)

3 tablespoons freshly
squeezed lemon juice
(about 1 lemon)

$1/2$ cup sugar

$1/4$ cup kirsch

This light dessert is a perfect ending to a winter's meal, especially when paired with Mocha-Rum Zabaglione and Chocolate-Peppercorn Cookies. Oranges may easily be substituted for tangerines.

Chill a rectangular metal baking pan (about 15 by 9 by 2 inches) in the freezer.

Strain the tangerine juice through a fine-meshed sieve into a large bowl. Add the zest, lemon juice, sugar, and kirsch and whisk until the sugar dissolves.

Pour the tangerine mixture into the chilled baking pan and freeze until ice crystals form around the sides and bottom of the pan, about 30 minutes. Carefully rake the mixture with a fork to loosen the ice crystals. Gently stir with the fork until the frozen and unfrozen elements are evenly combined. Do not break the crystals too finely, but do break up any large clumps that may have formed near the edges. Return to the freezer. Repeat this process every 20 minutes until the granita is the uniform consistency of soft crushed ice. This entire process will take about 2 hours in most freezers.

Serve immediately, or store in an airtight container in the freezer.

MAKES ABOUT 2 QUARTS

PEAR GRANITA

6 very ripe pears, peeled, cored, and cubed

²/₃ cup freshly squeezed lemon juice (about 4 lemons)

3 teaspoons grated lemon zest (about 2 lemons)

¹/₂ cup freshly squeezed orange juice (about 2 oranges)

¹/₂ teaspoon ground cinnamon

¹/₂ cup sugar

1 tablespoon plus 2 teaspoons pure vanilla extract

Ripe, juicy Bartlett pears are the best variety to use for this granita. Raspberry-Champagne Zabaglione makes an excellent topping, served with Almond Shortbread Cookies. It is also terrific topped with Mocha-Rum Zabaglione accompanied with Hazelnut Zebra Cookies.

Chill a rectangular metal baking pan (about 15 by 9 by 2 inches) in the freezer.

Fill a large saucepan one-third full with water. Bring to a gentle boil, then reduce heat to a simmer.

In a large metal bowl, combine the pears, lemon juice, lemon zest, orange juice,

cinnamon, and sugar. Set the bowl on top of the saucepan. Heat the fruit mixture until the sugar dissolves and the fruit has begun to give off its juices, about 15 minutes. Set aside to cool. In a blender or large-capacity food processor, purée the mixture until smooth. Strain the mixture through a fine-meshed sieve and stir in the vanilla.

Pour the pear mixture into the chilled baking pan and freeze until ice crystals form around the sides and bottom of the pan, about 30 minutes. Carefully rake the mixture with a fork to loosen the ice crystals. Gently stir with the fork until the frozen and unfrozen elements are evenly combined. Do not break the crystals too finely, but do break up any large clumps that may have formed near the edges. Return to the freezer. Repeat this process every 20 minutes until the granita is the uniform consistency of soft crushed ice. This entire process will take about 2 hours in most freezers.

Serve immediately, or store in an air-tight container in the freezer.

MAKES ABOUT 2 QUARTS

PINEAPPLE-RUM GRANITA

1 ripe pineapple, peeled, cored, and cut into 1-inch cubes

1/4 cup packed light brown sugar

3 tablespoons freshly squeezed lemon juice (about 1 lemon)

1/3 cup freshly squeezed orange juice (about 1 orange)

1 1/2 teaspoons grated lemon zest (about 1 lemon)

1 tablespoon grated orange zest (about 1 orange)

1 teaspoon pure vanilla extract

1/8 teaspoon salt

1/4 cup dark rum, such as Myers's

The native Caribbeans placed pineapples at the entrances to their homes as symbols of hospitality and promises of welcome and refreshment to all guests. Your guests will be truly refreshed by this tropical treat, especially when it is paired with Banana Caramel Sauce and Chocolate-Coconut Macaroons.

Chill a rectangular metal baking pan (about 15 by 9 by 2 inches) in the freezer.

Fill a large saucepan one-third full with water. Bring to a gentle boil, then reduce heat to a simmer.

In a large metal bowl, toss the pineapple with the brown sugar, lemon juice, and orange juice. Set the bowl on top of the saucepan. Cover the bowl with a tightly fitting lid or plastic wrap. Heat the pineapple until the sugar has dissolved and the fruit has begun to soften, about 20 minutes. Set aside to cool slightly.

In a blender or large-capacity food processor, purée the fruit until smooth. Pass through a food mill or coarse-meshed sieve back into the bowl. Stir in the lemon zest, orange zest, vanilla extract, salt, and rum. Cover and refrigerate for 1 hour.

Pour the pineapple mixture into the chilled baking pan and freeze until ice crystals form around the sides and bottom of the pan, about 30 minutes. Carefully rake the mixture with a fork to loosen the ice crystals. Gently stir with the fork until the frozen and unfrozen elements are evenly combined. Do not break the crystals too finely, but do break up any large clumps that may form near the edges. Return to the freezer. Repeat this process every 20 minutes until the granita is the uniform consistency of soft crushed ice. This entire process will take about 2 hours in most freezers.

Serve immediately or store in an airtight container in the freezer.

MAKES ABOUT 2 QUARTS

WATERMELON GRANITA

3 pounds watermelon, scraped from rind, seeded, and cut into small chunks (about 5 cups fruit)

1/2 cup freshly squeezed lemon juice (about 3 lemons)

1/4 cup sugar

3 tablespoons Campari

1/8 teaspoon salt

Campari is an Italian aperitif that is a natural digestive. It is made using a secret formula whose ingredients include bitter and fragrant seeds, flowers, leaves, roots, and stems in an alcohol base.

Serve this colorful icy delight alone or with Mint Zabaglione and Pecan Sandies for a sensational summertime treat.

Chill a rectangular metal baking pan (about 15 by 9 by 2 inches) in the freezer.

In a blender or large-capacity food processor, purée the watermelon, lemon juice, and sugar until smooth. Stir in the Campari and salt.

Pour the watermelon mixture into the chilled baking pan and freeze until ice crystals form around the sides and bottom of the pan, about 30 minutes. Carefully rake the mixture with a fork to loosen the ice crystals. Gently stir with the fork until the frozen and unfrozen elements are evenly combined. Do not break the crystals too finely, but do break up any large clumps that may form near the edges. Return to the freezer. Repeat this process every 20 minutes until the granita is the uniform consistency of soft crushed ice. This entire process will take about 2 hours in most freezers.

Serve immediately, or store in an airtight container in the freezer.

MAKES ABOUT 2 QUARTS

Sauces

Chef John Dudek has mastered the art of pairing delectable sauces with simple granitas to make exceptional desserts. These luscious sauces combine a few basic ingredients with wonderful results.

The majority of the sauce recipes in this section are variations on the traditional Italian dessert zabaglione; they combine flavored custard with whipped cream. Their smooth texture perfectly complements icy granita. These sauces are also elegant accompaniments to fresh fruit or simple cakes, or may be eaten alone as truly decadent desserts.

Apricot-Tea Infusion and Banana Caramel and Black Currant–Cabernet sauces are richly hued toppings that may be served with granita, ice cream, poached fruit, or a slice of plain cake.

Each recipe includes recommendations for serving with specific granitas, along with alternative serving suggestions. Once you have mastered these exceptional sauces you can allow your inspiration to guide you in making other pairings.

For ease of preparation, the recipes indicate how far in advance of serving the sauces may be made—a few hours in some cases, several days in others. Each recipe produces enough sauce for 8 servings (about 2 quarts) of granita.

APRICOT-TEA INFUSION

1/2 cup tightly packed
  dried apricots

2 1/2 cups water

1 1/2 cups freshly squeezed
  orange juice (about
  5 oranges)

1/2 cup sugar

1 tea bag Orange Pekoe or
  other black tea

*Look for dried apricots
prepared without sulfur,
available in natural
foods stores.*

Spoon this tangy sweet sauce over Cherry Granita or your favorite ice cream.

In a small saucepan, combine the apricots, 1 1/2 cups of the water, the orange juice, and sugar. Bring to a boil, then reduce heat and simmer until the apricots are tender, about 20 minutes. Remove from heat and transfer to a small bowl. Add the tea bag and let steep for 5 minutes. Remove the tea bag, squeezing out all the liquid. Place the sauce into a blender or large-capacity food processor. Add the remaining 1 cup water and purée to a smooth, pourable sauce. Strain through a fine-meshed sieve and let cool to room temperature. The sauce may thicken as it cools and can be thinned with water as necessary.

To store, cover and refrigerate for up to 1 week. Bring the sauce to room temperature before serving.

MAKES 1 1/2 CUPS

BANANA CARAMEL SAUCE

2 very ripe bananas, peeled and thinly sliced

1/4 teaspoon ground cinnamon

1 teaspoon grated lemon zest (about 1 lemon)

1 teaspoon grated orange zest (about 1/2 orange)

1/2 tablespoon pure vanilla extract

11/2 tablespoons dark rum, such as Myers's

1/2 cup sugar

11/2 cups freshly squeezed orange juice (about 5 oranges)

Fragrant bananas and dark rum make a delicious sauce to serve over Pineapple-Rum Granita or vanilla ice cream.

In a medium bowl, toss the bananas with the cinnamon, lemon zest, orange zest, vanilla extract, and rum. Set aside.

Put the sugar in a medium-sized heavy saucepan. Place over medium-high heat and cook, stirring with a wooden spoon, until the sugar has melted and turned an amber color, about 5 to 7 minutes. Remove from heat and carefully add the orange juice in a slow, steady stream while stirring constantly. Place the saucepan over very low heat and stir until the mixture is smooth.

Carefully spoon the banana mixture into the saucepan. Bring to a simmer and cook for 10 minutes, stirring occasionally. Set aside to cool.

Pour the mixture into a blender or large-capacity food processor. Purée until smooth and strain through a fine-meshed sieve. Keep tightly covered until ready to serve. The sauce may thicken as it cools and can be thinned with orange juice or water as necessary. To store, refrigerate in an airtight container for up to 1 week. Return to room temperature before serving.

MAKES 11/2 CUPS

BEAUMES DE VENISE ZABAGLIONE

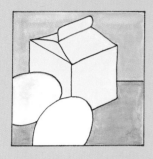

Beaumes de Venise is a French dessert wine similar to Sauternes. It is golden in color, with a pleasant, not too sweet flavor. Excellent varieties are also produced in California. A 350 mL bottle may be used when preparing this recipe. Serve this sauce with Honeydew or Pink Grapefruit granita.

4 egg yolks

1/4 cup sugar

1 teaspoon grated orange zest (about 1/2 orange)

1/2 cup Beaumes de Venise wine

1 cup heavy cream

Prepare a double boiler.

In the bowl of an electric mixer beat the egg yolks and sugar until thick and pale in color. Scrape down the sides of the bowl with a rubber spatula and whisk in the orange zest and Beaumes de Venise. Transfer the mixture to a double boiler and whisk constantly over barely simmering water for about 5 to 7 minutes, or until it thickens to a smooth, glossy custard. Remove from heat, cover, and refrigerate for at least 1 hour.

In a deep bowl, beat the cream until it forms soft peaks. Using a rubber spatula, fold the chilled custard into the whipped cream. Serve immediately, or cover and refrigerate for up to 3 hours.

MAKES 3 CUPS

BLACK CURRANT–
CABERNET SAUCE

1 cup Cabernet
   Sauvignon wine

1 cup freshly squeezed
   orange juice (about
   3 oranges)

1/4 cup sugar

1 teaspoon grated lemon
   zest (about 1/2 lemon)

1 teaspoon grated orange
   zest (about 1/2 orange)

1 star anise pod

1/2 cup black currant syrup

*Black currant syrup
is a nonalcoholic syrup
made from fresh fruit
and very little sugar.
Look for D'Arbo
syrups, produced in
Austria and sold in
specialty foods stores.*

*This rich red sauce is simple to prepare.
Each savory taste reveals layers of flavors
that are especially well paired with Pink
Grapefruit or Green Apple granita.*

In a medium saucepan, combine the Cabernet, orange juice, sugar, lemon and orange zests, and star anise. Bring to a boil, then reduce heat and simmer for 15 minutes. Remove from heat, cover tightly, and let sit until cool, about 45 minutes.

Strain the mixture through a fine-meshed sieve and discard the star anise. Stir in the black currant syrup. Refrigerate until 1 hour before serving. This sauce may be stored in the refrigerator for up to 1 week.

MAKES 2 CUPS

BLACKBERRY ZABAGLIONE

2 cups fresh blackberries

4 egg yolks

$^1/_4$ cup sugar

1 tablespoon freshly
squeezed lemon juice
(about 1 lemon)

1 teaspoon grated lemon
zest (about $^1/_2$ lemon)

2 tablespoons Chambord
liqueur

1 cup heavy cream

*Chambord is a
raspberry liqueur that
is principally
produced in France.*

*Try this beautiful creamy purple sauce over
Lime-Mint Granita. Or, simply serve a
dollop on a bowl of mixed summer berries.
Frozen blackberries may be substituted
for fresh.*

Put the blackberries in a blender or food
processor. Purée until smooth. Strain the
purée through a fine-meshed sieve into a
large bowl. Set aside.

Prepare a double boiler.

In the bowl of an electric mixer, beat
the egg yolks and sugar until they are thick
and pale in color. Scrape down the sides of
the bowl with a rubber spatula and whisk
in the lemon juice, lemon zest, Chambord,
and blackberry purée. Transfer the mixture
to a double boiler and whisk constantly
over barely simmering water for about 5 to
7 minutes or until it thickens to a smooth,
glossy custard. Remove from heat, cover,
and refrigerate for at least 1 hour.

In a deep bowl, beat the cream until it
forms soft peaks. Using a rubber spatula,
fold the chilled custard into the whipped
cream. Serve immediately, or cover and
refrigerate for up to 3 hours.

MAKES 3 CUPS

BURNT SUGAR AND CALVADOS ZABAGLIONE

1/2 plus 1/4 cup sugar

1 1/2 tablespoons water

4 egg yolks

1 1/2 teaspoons grated lemon zest (about 1 lemon)

1/2 teaspoon pure vanilla extract

1/8 teaspoon ground nutmeg

1 tablespoon Calvados

1 cup heavy cream

Calvados is a variety of apple brandy or apple jack distilled in France and America from crisp cider apples. There is not an exact substitute for Calvados, but nonalcoholic still cider may be substituted in this sauce.

Calvados adds a delicious flavor to this special sauce. It complements Green Apple Granita magnificently and also makes a sophisticated accent for a piece of spice cake.

Put the 1/4 cup of sugar in a small, heavy saucepan and stir over medium heat until the sugar has melted and turned a deep amber color, about 5 minutes. Reduce heat to low and carefully and slowly stir in the water to form a smooth caramel syrup. Set aside to cool slightly.

Prepare a double boiler.

In the bowl of an electric mixer, beat the egg yolks and the remaining 1/2 cup sugar until thick and pale in color. Scrape down the sides of the bowl with a rubber spatula and whisk in the lemon zest, vanilla, nutmeg, and cooled caramel syrup. Transfer the mixture to the double boiler and whisk constantly over barely simmering water for about 5 to 7 minutes, or until it thickens to a smooth, glossy custard. Remove from heat, cover, and refrigerate for at least 1 hour.

Stir the Calvados into the custard. In a deep bowl, beat the cream until it forms soft peaks. Using a rubber spatula, fold the chilled custard into the whipped cream. Serve immediately, or cover and refrigerate for up to 3 hours.

MAKES 3 CUPS

LEMON-CHARDONNAY ZABAGLIONE

4 egg yolks

1/4 cup sugar

1 tablespoon freshly
squeezed lemon juice
(about 1/2 lemon)

1 teaspoon grated lemon
zest (about 1 lemon)

1/2 teaspoon pure vanilla
extract

1/2 cup Chardonnay wine

1 cup heavy cream

This lightly flavored zabaglione is excellent served over Nectarine Granita or sliced fresh fruit.

Prepare a double boiler.

In the bowl of an electric mixer, beat the egg yolks and sugar until thick and pale in color. Scrape down the sides of the bowl and whisk in the lemon juice, lemon zest, and vanilla. Scrape down the sides of the bowl and stir in the Chardonnay. Transfer the mixture to the double boiler and whisk constantly over barely simmering water for about 5 to 7 minutes, or until thickened to a smooth, glossy custard. Remove from the heat, cover, and refrigerate for at least 1 hour.

In a deep bowl, beat the cream until it forms soft peaks. Using a rubber spatula, fold the chilled custard into the whipped cream. Serve immediately, or cover and refrigerate for up to 3 hours.

MAKES 3 CUPS

MINT ZABAGLIONE

1/2 cup packed mint leaves
1/4 cup sugar
1/2 cup dry white wine
4 egg yolks
1 cup heavy cream

This beautiful sauce, delicately flecked with mint, is delicious with Watermelon Granita, sliced fresh fruit, or even a slice of chocolate cake.

Combine the mint leaves and sugar in a blender or food processor. Purée while adding the white wine in a steady stream. Set aside.

Prepare a double boiler.

In the bowl of an electric mixer, beat the egg yolks until thick and pale in color. Scrape down the sides of the bowl with a rubber spatula and whisk in the mint mixture. Transfer to a double boiler and whisk constantly over barely simmering water for about 5 to 7 minutes, or until it thickens to a smooth, glossy custard. Remove from heat, cover, and refrigerate for at least 1 hour.

In a deep bowl, beat the cream until it forms soft peaks. Using a rubber spatula, fold the chilled custard into the whipped cream. Serve immediately, or cover and refrigerate for up to 3 hours.

MAKES 3 CUPS

MOCHA-RUM ZABAGLIONE

4 egg yolks

2¹/₂ tablespoons sugar

¹/₂ cup freshly brewed espresso coffee, cooled

1¹/₂ ounces bittersweet chocolate, grated

1¹/₂ tablespoons dark rum

1 teaspoon grated orange zest (about ¹/₂ orange)

1 teaspoon pure vanilla extract

1 cup heavy cream

The word mocha, *which has come to mean the combination of coffee and chocolate, is derived from the name of the Arabian city where the English and the Dutch East India Companies set up coffee trading in the early 1600s. Serve a dollop of this light sauce, which is a heavenly combination of these flavors, over Tangerine Granita or Pear Granita.*

Prepare a double boiler.

In the bowl of an electric mixer, beat the egg yolks and sugar until thick and pale in color. Scrape down the sides of the bowl with a rubber spatula and whisk in the espresso coffee. Transfer the mixture to a double boiler and whisk constantly over barely simmering water for about 5 to 7 minutes, until it thickens to a smooth, glossy custard. Remove from heat and whisk in the chocolate, rum, orange zest, and vanilla until fully incorporated. Cover and refrigerate for at least 1 hour.

In a deep bowl, beat the cream until it forms soft peaks. Using a rubber spatula, fold the chilled custard into the whipped cream. Serve immediately, or cover and refrigerate for up to 3 hours.

MAKES 3 CUPS

63

RASPBERRY-CHAMPAGNE ZABAGLIONE

1 cup fresh raspberries

1 cup heavy cream

4 egg yolks

1/4 cup sugar

1/2 cup champagne

1/8 cup brandy

2 tablespoons freshly squeezed lemon juice (about 1 lemon)

1 teaspoon grated lemon zest (about 1 lemon)

Present this beautiful zabaglione over Lemon Granita served in clear glass goblets. For a striking visual and taste sensation, consider serving this sauce over lemon-flavored cake. You may substitute thawed frozen raspberries for fresh.

Put the raspberries in a blender or food processor and purée until smooth. Strain the purée through a fine-meshed sieve into a metal bowl. Place the sieve full of raspberry seeds over the bowl and pour the cream over the raspberry seeds to extract any additional raspberry flavor and coloring. Cover and refrigerate.

Prepare a double boiler.

In the bowl of an electric mixer, beat the egg yolks and sugar until thick and pale in color. Scrape down the sides of the bowl with a rubber spatula and whisk in the champagne, brandy, lemon juice, and lemon zest. Transfer the mixture to the double boiler and whisk constantly over barely simmering water for about 5 to 7 minutes, or until it thickens to a smooth, glossy custard. Remove from heat, cover, and refrigerate for at least 1 hour.

In a deep bowl, beat the cream and raspberry purée until soft peaks form. Using a rubber spatula, fold the chilled custard into the whipped cream. Serve immediately, or cover and refrigerate for up to 3 hours.

MAKES 3 CUPS

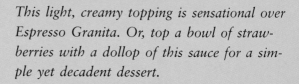

STRAWBERRY ZABAGLIONE

1/2 cup quartered hulled strawberries

1/4 cup plus 3 tablespoons sugar

4 egg yolks

2 teaspoons freshly squeezed lemon juice (about 1/2 lemon)

1 teaspoon grated lemon zest (about 1 lemon)

1 tablespoon kirsch

1 cup heavy cream

This light, creamy topping is sensational over Espresso Granita. Or, top a bowl of strawberries with a dollop of this sauce for a simple yet decadent dessert.

Prepare a double boiler.

Combine the strawberries and the 3 tablespoons sugar in a double boiler and cook over simmering water, stirring occasionally, until the fruit is tender, about five minutes. Remove from heat and let cool. Purée the fruit in a blender or food processor until smooth, about 1 minute.

In the bowl of an electric mixer, beat the egg yolks and sugar until thick and pale in color. Scrape down the sides of the bowl with a rubber spatula and whisk in the lemon juice, lemon zest, kirsch, and strawberry purée. Transfer the mixture to the double boiler and whisk constantly over barely simmering water for about 5 to 7 minutes, or until it thickens to a smooth, glossy custard. Remove from heat, cover, and refrigerate for at least 1 hour.

In a deep bowl, beat the cream until it forms soft peaks. Using a rubber spatula, fold the chilled custard into the whipped cream. Serve immediately, or cover and refrigerate for up to 3 hours.

MAKES 3 CUPS

Cookies

The cookies in this section make special desserts all by themselves, or they can be served as elegant accompaniments to sorbets, granitas, and sauces—as they are at Duane Park Cafe. They are all easy to prepare, store well, and will greatly enhance every baker's repertoire.

Three of the recipes are for biscotti, which originated in Italy (the word *biscotti* means "twice-baked") and are perfect to serve with granita or zabaglione. They are also delicious served with coffee or for dipping into a glass of dessert wine.

Almond Shortbread Cookies, Cardamom-Orange Cookies, Chocolate-Coconut Macaroons, Chocolate Peppercorn Cookies, and Pecan Sandies are traditional cookies with a twist. While their preparation is easy, their flavors are complex. Thanks to the simple addition of ingredients such as citrus zest, spices, or extracts, these cookies are sophisticated dessert fare. Delicately curved Cinnamon Walnut Tuiles and abstractly striped Hazelnut Zebra Cookies combine terrific flavor with a professional presentation.

CARDAMOM-ORANGE COOKIES

1 cup butter, softened

1/4 cup granulated sugar

1 egg yolk

4 1/2 teaspoons ground
cardamom

2 tablespoons grated
orange zest (about
2 oranges)

1 1/2 teaspoons pure
vanilla extract

1/8 teaspoon salt

2 cups flour

1/4 cup confectioners'
sugar

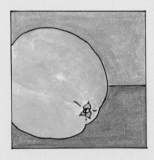

Cardamom, a member of the ginger family, adds a warm, spicy-sweet flavor to these cookies. Their subtle flavor pairs well with fruit-based sorbets and granitas.

In the bowl of an electric mixture, cream the butter and granulated sugar until light and fluffy. Scrape down the sides of the bowl with a rubber spatula, add the egg yolk, and continue beating until thoroughly mixed. Beat in the cardamom, orange zest, vanilla extract, and salt. On low speed, add the flour, scraping the bowl with the spatula and beating only until smooth. Cover the dough with plastic wrap and refrigerate for 1 hour.

Dust your hands lightly with flour and roll tablespoon-sized portions of the dough between your palms to form 1-inch balls. Place 2 inches apart on the baking sheet and refrigerate for 15 minutes. Preheat the oven to 350° and line a baking sheet with parchment or grease it.

With flour-dusted fingertips, flatten each cookie ball to a 1/4-inch thickness. Bake for about 12 minutes, or until lightly browned. Let cool completely on the baking sheet. The cookies may be stored in an airtight container for up to 4 days. Dust with confectioners' sugar before serving.

MAKES 24 COOKIES

BLUEBERRY-ALMOND BISCOTTI

1 cup dried blueberries

1/4 cup kirsch

1 tablespoon grated lemon zest (about 2 lemons)

1 3/4 cups flour

1/2 teaspoon baking powder

1/2 teaspoon baking soda

1/8 teaspoon salt

1 1/2 cups (8 ounces) blanched or unblanched almonds

1/2 cup butter, softened

1 cup sugar

2 eggs

1 1/2 teaspoons pure vanilla extract

This recipe makes 6-inch-long biscotti. If you prefer a shorter version, shape the dough into two 15 by 2 1/2 by 1-inch logs and proceed with the recipe as written. This version will yield 36 biscotti.

Dried blueberries may be found in most grocery stores or can be ordered by mail. Consult the Ingredient Sources for further information.

In a small bowl, combine the blueberries, kirsch, and lemon zest. Let sit for 2 hours.

Sift together the flour, baking powder, baking soda, and salt. Set aside. Grind 1/2 cup of the almonds in a blender, food processor, or nut grinder until finely ground.

In the bowl of an electric mixer, cream the butter and sugar until light and fluffy, scraping down the sides with a rubber spatula as necessary. Beat in the eggs one at a time. Mix in the vanilla. With the mixer set on low, add the blueberry mixture. Stir in the sifted ingredients until blended. Stir in the whole and ground nuts until blended.

Turn the dough out onto a sheet of plastic wrap about 18 inches long. Loosely cover with another long sheet of plastic wrap and form the dough into a 15 by 5-inch log that is 1 inch thick. Wrap the dough tightly in the plastic wrap and refrigerate for 30 to 40 minutes, or until firm.

Preheat the oven to 350° and line a baking sheet with parchment paper or grease it. Unwrap the dough, place it on the pan, and bake for 30 minutes, or until firm and golden brown. Remove from the oven and let cool on the baking sheet for 15 minutes.

Lower the oven temperature to 275°. Transfer the cooled log to a cutting board. Using a serrated knife, score the log on the diagonal at 3/4-inch intervals, then cut all the way through the scored lines to make slices. Return the slices to the baking sheet, cut-side down. Bake for 10 minutes on each side, or until dry and lightly browned. Transfer the biscotti to wire racks and let cool completely. Store in an airtight container for up to 1 week.

MAKES 24 BISCOTTI

PISTACHIO BISCOTTI

1³/₄ cups flour

¹/₂ teaspoon baking soda

¹/₂ teaspoon baking powder

¹/₈ teaspoon salt

1¹/₂ cups (6 ounces) unsalted pistachios

¹/₂ cup butter, softened

1 cup sugar

2 eggs

2 teaspoons grated lemon zest (about 1 lemon)

2 teaspoons grated orange zest (about 1 orange)

1 tablespoon pure vanilla extract

1 tablespoon kirsch

This recipe makes 6-inch-long biscotti. If you prefer a shorter version, shape the dough into two 15 by 2¹/₂-inch logs, each 1 inch thick, and proceed with the recipe as written. This version will yield 36 biscotti.

Pistachio nuts add a delicate, pale green color to these delicious cookies. Look for shelled pistachios in jars at the grocery store, or purchase a pound of nuts in the shell.

Sift together the flour, baking soda, baking powder, and salt. Set aside. Finely chop ¹/₂ cup of the pistachios and set aside.

In the bowl of an electric mixer, cream the butter and sugar until light and fluffy, scraping down the sides with a rubber spatula as needed. Beat in the eggs one at a time. Add the lemon zest, orange zest, vanilla extract, and kirsch. Lower the speed and add the sifted ingredients. Stir in the whole and finely chopped nuts to combine.

Turn the dough out onto a sheet of plastic wrap about 18 inches long. Loosely cover with another long sheet of plastic wrap and form the dough into a 15 by 5-inch log that is 1 inch thick. Wrap the dough tightly in the plastic wrap and refrigerate for 30 to 40 minutes, or until firm.

Preheat the oven to 350° and line a baking sheet with parchment paper or grease it. Unwrap the log, place it on the prepared pan, and bake for 30 minutes, or until firm and golden brown. Remove from the oven and allow to cool on the baking sheet for 15 minutes.

Lower the oven temperature to 275°. Transfer the cooled log to a cutting board. Using a serrated knife, score the log on the diagonal at 3/4-inch intervals. Cut through the scored lines to make slices. Place the slices on the baking sheet, cut side down. Bake for 10 minutes on each side, until dry and lightly browned. Transfer to wire racks to cool completely. Store in an airtight container for up to 1 week.

MAKES 24 BISCOTTI

CHOCOLATE–MACADAMIA NUT BISCOTTI

2 cups flour

1¹/₂ teaspoons baking powder

1 teaspoon salt

1 cup butter, softened

1 cup sugar

2 eggs

1 tablespoon grated orange zest (about 1 orange)

1 tablespoon pure vanilla extract

1 tablespoon dark crème de cacao or Kahlúa

1¹/₂ cups macadamia nuts, coarsely chopped (one 7-ounce jar)

1 cup coarsely chopped bittersweet chocolate (about 8 ounces)

This recipe makes 6-inch-long biscotti. If you prefer a shorter version, shape the dough into two 15 by 2¹/₂-inch logs that are 1 inch thick and proceed with the recipe as written. This will yield 36 biscotti.

Rich in flavor, these macadamia-studded, chocolate-flecked biscotti are truly luxurious!

Sift together the flour, baking powder, and salt. Set aside.

In the bowl of an electric mixer, cream the butter and sugar until light and fluffy, scraping down the sides of the bowl with a rubber spatula as needed. Beat in the eggs one at a time. Beat in the orange zest, vanilla extract, and crème de cacao. Lower the speed and beat in the sifted ingredients. Stir in the nuts and chocolate until blended.

Turn the dough out onto a sheet of plastic wrap about 18 inches long. Loosely cover with another sheet and form the dough into a 15 by 5-inch log that is 1 inch thick. Wrap the log tightly in the plastic wrap and refrigerate for 30 to 40 minutes, or until firm.

Preheat the oven to 350°. Line a baking sheet with parchment paper or grease it. Remove the plastic from the log and transfer the log to the prepared pan. Bake the log for 30 minutes, or until firm and golden brown. Let cool on the baking sheet for 15 minutes.

Lower the oven temperature to 275°. Transfer the cooled log to a cutting board.

Using a serrated knife, score the log on the diagonal at $3/4$-inch intervals, then cut through the scored lines to make slices. Place the slices on the baking sheet, cut side down. Bake for 10 minutes on each side, or until dry and lightly browned. Transfer the biscotti to wire racks and let cool completely. Store in an airtight container for up to 1 week.

MAKES 24 BISCOTTI

ALMOND SHORTBREAD COOKIES

1 cup (5 1/2 ounces)
  unblanched almonds

1 cup butter, softened

1/2 cup granulated sugar

1/4 cup cornstarch

1 1/2 teaspoons pure vanilla
  extract

1/2 teaspoon pure almond
  extract

2 teaspoons grated lemon
  zest (about 1 lemon)

2 cups flour

1/4 cup confectioners'
  sugar

This cookie has a great buttery almond flavor with a shortbread crispness. Blanched almonds may be substituted for unblanched, if you like.

Finely grind 1/2 cup of the almonds in a blender, food processor, or nut grinder. Coarsely grind the remaining 1/2 cup of almonds. Set aside.

In the bowl of an electric mixer, cream the butter until light and fluffy. Scrape down the sides of the bowl with a rubber spatula and add the granulated sugar, blending until smooth. On low speed, work in the finely ground almonds, cornstarch, vanilla extract, almond extract, and lemon zest, scraping down the sides of the bowl and blending until just incorporated. Finally, add the flour, stirring on low speed until the ingredients begin to form a ball. Wrap the dough in plastic and refrigerate for 30 minutes.

Roll the dough between 2 pieces of parchment or waxed paper to an even 1/4-inch thick rectangle that will fit your baking sheet (about 15 by 9 inches). Slide the dough, sandwiched in the paper, onto a baking sheet and refrigerate for 30 minutes, or until cold and firm.

Peel away the top layer of paper and evenly coat the dough with the coarsely ground almonds. Dust a rolling pin with flour and roll it across the almond-coated surface until the nuts are embedded in the dough. Refrigerate for 15 minutes. Meanwhile, preheat the oven to 350°.

Use a knife to score the dough in horizontal rows 2 inches apart. Then score the dough on the diagonal in rows 3 inches apart to create a series of elongated diamond shapes. Bake for 10 minutes, or until lightly browned. Remove from the oven and re-score on the same lines. Return to the oven and bake for 10 to 15 minutes, or until golden brown.

Let cool for 10 minutes. While still warm, use a long sharp knife to cut through each scored line. Let cool completely. The cookies may be stored in an airtight container for up to 1 week. Dust with confectioners' sugar just before serving.

MAKES 36 COOKIES

CHOCOLATE-COCONUT
MACAROONS

8 ounces bittersweet
  chocolate, chopped

¹/₃ cup hot freshly brewed
  coffee

1 tablespoon pure vanilla
  extract

1¹/₂ cups (8 ounces)
  blanched or unblanched
  almonds, finely ground

¹/₂ cup granulated sugar

1 tablespoon flour

2 egg whites

¹/₈ teaspoon salt

¹/₈ teaspoon cream of
  tartar

¹/₄ cup confectioners'
  sugar

2 to 3 cups unsweetened
  shredded coconut

*Freida's unsweetened
shredded coconut
(which is excellent) is
widely carried in
grocery stores and is
also available by mail
(see Ingredient Sources).*

*Macaroon lovers will delight in this unique
variation on a traditional cookie. Sweetened
coconut flakes may be substituted for
unsweetened shredded coconut.*

Melt the chocolate in a double boiler set
over barely simmering water. Stir in the hot
coffee and vanilla and set aside to cool. In a
medium bowl, combine the ground almonds,
granulated sugar, and flour. Set aside.

   In the bowl of an electric mixer, combine the egg whites, salt, and cream of tartar.
Beat until the egg whites hold a soft peak.
Beat in the confectioners' sugar. Using a rubber spatula, fold the chocolate mixture into
the egg whites just until barely incorporated.
Fold in half of the almond mixture until
barely incorporated. Fold in the remaining
almond mixture. Cover with plastic wrap and
refrigerate for 30 minutes, or until firm.

   Preheat the oven to 325°. Line a baking
sheet with parchment paper or grease it.
Place the shredded coconut in a shallow
bowl. Shape the dough into mounds about
1 inch in diameter. Gently roll the dough in
the coconut to coat. Transfer to the prepared
baking sheet, placing the mounds 1 inch
apart. Bake for 15 minutes, or until firm. Let
cool on the baking sheet. Store in an airtight
container for up to 4 days.

MAKES 32 COOKIES

CHOCOLATE-PEPPERCORN
COOKIES

¾ cup butter, softened

1 cup sugar

1 egg

1 tablespoon pure vanilla
extract

1 teaspoon grated orange
zest (about 1 orange)

1½ cups flour

¾ cup unsweetened cocoa
powder

¼ teaspoon salt

¼ teaspoon finely ground
black pepper

¼ teaspoon cayenne
pepper

¾ teaspoon ground
cinnamon

*This dough may also
be rolled out and cut
with cookie cutters.
Divide the dough in
half, wrap in plastic
wrap, and refrigerate
for 30 minutes. Roll
each half between
pieces of parchment or
waxed paper to a
¼-inch thickness.
Refrigerate for 10 min-
utes before cutting into
shapes and baking.*

*This variation of a traditional Mexican cookie
has a subtle orange flavor and a lot of zing!*

In the bowl of an electric mixer, cream the
butter and sugar until light and fluffy. Scrape
down the sides of the bowl with a rubber
spatula and add the egg, vanilla, and orange
zest. Beat on medium speed for 5 minutes.

Sift together the flour, cocoa powder,
salt, black pepper, cayenne, and cinnamon.
Reduce the speed to low and gradually add
the dry ingredients, scraping down the sides
as needed and beating just until mixed.

Turn the dough out onto a sheet of plastic wrap about 14 inches long and cover it
loosely with the plastic wrap. With the palms
of your hands, roll the dough into a 1½-inch-
diameter log. Wrap the dough completely in
plastic wrap and refrigerate until firm, about
30 minutes.

Preheat the oven to 325°. Line a baking
sheet with parchment paper or grease it.

Slice the chilled log into ¼-inch-thick
slices and arrange them 1½ inches apart on
the prepared baking sheet. Bake for 12 to
15 minutes, or until the cookies are firm to
the touch. Let cool on the baking sheet for
5 minutes, then transfer to racks to cool
completely. Store in an airtight container for
up to 1 week.

MAKES ABOUT 40 COOKIES

CINNAMON-WALNUT TUILES

1/2 cup sugar

1/3 cup heavy cream

1/3 cup honey

2 tablespoons butter

1 teaspoon ground
cinnamon

1 1/2 cups (6 ounces) walnuts, finely chopped

*These delicate curled cookies look very pro-
fessional but are quite easy to make. To
ensure the success of this recipe, we highly
recommend using parchment-lined heavy
baking sheets.*

In a small, heavy saucepan, combine the
sugar, heavy cream, honey, butter, and cinnamon. Cook over medium heat, stirring with
a wooden spoon, until the mixture comes to
a boil. Remove from heat and let cool
slightly. Stir in the walnuts and set aside. Let
cool completely.

Preheat the oven to 400°. Line a heavy
baking sheet with parchment paper. Spoon
out rounded teaspoons of batter, slightly
flattening each mound, 2 inches apart on the
prepared baking sheet. Bake for 8 to 10
minutes, or until a rich, caramel color. Let
cool only slightly. Carefully lift each warm
cookie with a spatula and lay across a
curved surface such as a rolling pin or small
glass placed on its side. Let cool completely
into a curved shape. Stored in an airtight
container for up to 4 days.

MAKES 24 COOKIES

PECAN SANDIES

1/2 cup butter, softened
1/4 cup granulated sugar
1 cup finely ground pecans
1 1/2 teaspoons pure vanilla
  extract
1 teaspoon grated lemon
  zest (about 1 lemon)
1 1/2 cups flour
1/2 cup confectioners'
  sugar

This light and wonderful cookie, inspired by several traditional recipes, will melt in your mouth!

Preheat the oven to 325°. Line a baking sheet with parchment paper or grease it.

In the bowl of an electric mixer, cream the butter and granulated sugar until light and fluffy, about 5 minutes. Scrape down the sides of the bowl with a rubber spatula. Add the pecans, mixing on low speed until incorporated. Stir in the vanilla and lemon zest. Add the flour, mixing until a loose dough forms.

Roll tablespoon-sized portions of the dough between your palms to form 1-inch balls. Place the balls 2 inches apart on the prepared baking sheet. Refrigerate for 10 minutes.

Bake the cookies for 18 to 20 minutes, or until barely golden with lightly browned bottoms. Let cool for 5 minutes on the baking sheet, then transfer to wire racks. These cookies may be stored in an airtight container for up to 1 week, but do not stack them too high or they will break. Roll each cookie in the confectioners' sugar just before serving.

MAKES 20 COOKIES

HAZELNUT ZEBRA COOKIES

2 cups (10 ounces)
hazelnuts

2 cups flour

1 cup butter, softened

$1/2$ cup granulated sugar

2 tablespoons pure
vanilla extract

$1/8$ teaspoon pure
almond extract

2 teaspoons grated lemon
zest (about 1 lemon)

$1/4$ cup confectioners'
sugar

6 ounces bittersweet
chocolate, melted

*A small self-sealing
plastic bag may
substitute for the pastry
bag. Just fill with the
chocolate, seal the bag,
and cut a small hole
in one bottom corner,
then squeeze out the
chocolate.*

No one can resist these chocolate-striped nutty delights. Decorate the cookies on the day you plan to serve them. Undecorated cookies may be stored in an airtight container for up to 4 days.

Coarsely chop the hazelnuts and toss with the flour. Set aside.

In the bowl of an electric mixer, cream the butter and granulated sugar until light and fluffy, about 5 minutes. Scrape down the sides of the bowl with a rubber spatula. Add the vanilla extract, almond extract, and lemon zest, mixing on low speed to blend. Beat in the hazelnut mixture until incorporated. With a rubber spatula, scrape the dough into a ball, cover with plastic wrap, and refrigerate until firm, about 30 minutes.

Preheat the oven to 350°. Line a baking sheet with parchment paper or grease it. Roll tablespoon-sized portions of dough between your palms to form walnut-sized balls. Place the balls 2 inches apart on the prepared baking sheet and refrigerate for 15 minutes. Bake for 18 minutes, or until barely golden with lightly browned bottoms. Cool completely on wire racks.

Line a baking sheet with waxed paper or parchment. Arrange the cookies close together but not touching on the baking sheet. Using a fine-meshed sieve, dust the confectioners' sugar evenly over the tops of the cookies. Spoon the melted chocolate into a pastry bag fitted with a small plain pastry tip (No. 4). Scribble chocolate over each cookie to create alternating zebra stripes of white sugar and dark chocolate. Refrigerate the cookies for 5 minutes to set the chocolate.

MAKES 30 COOKIES

GARNISHES · EQUIPMENT · INGREDIENT

SOURCES · BIOGRAPHIES · INDEX ·

GARNISHES · EQUIPMENT · INGREDIENT

SOURCES · BIOGRAPHIES · INDEX ·

GARNISHES · EQUIPMENT · INGREDIENT

SOURCES · BIOGRAPHIES · INDEX ·

GARNISHES · EQUIPMENT · INGREDIENT

SOURCES · BIOGRAPHIES · INDEX ·

GARNISHES · EQUIPMENT · INGREDIENT

SOURCES · BIOGRAPHIES · INDEX ·

GARNISHES · EQUIPMENT · INGREDIENT

SOURCES · BIOGRAPHIES · INDEX

GARNISHES

EDIBLE FLOWERS AND HERBS

Duane Park Cafe serves sorbets and granitas garnished with sprigs of fresh herbs, such as mint, and edible flowers. Some suitable flowers include peppery nasturtiums, delicate violets and pansies, colorful calendula, and soft rose petals. Make sure the flowers and herbs are unsprayed.

CITRUS ZEST

Grapefruit, lemon, lime, and orange zests make colorful garnishes for sorbets and granitas. A sharp knife or vegetable peeler can be used to remove long strips of peel. Cut the strips into very thin slices with a sharp knife and use to decorate individual portions of dessert. Or, use a zester to make fine curls.

CANDIED CITRUS PEEL

Candied citrus peel is both decorative and edible. It will keep for several weeks if stored in the refrigerator.

4^1/$_3$ cups water

1^1/$_2$ cups loosely packed assorted strips citrus peel

1 cup sugar

In a large saucepan, bring 4 cups of the water to a boil. Add the citrus zest and simmer for 8 to 10 minutes. Drain, rinse under cold water, and set aside. Place the remaining ^{1}/$_3$ cup water and the sugar in a small saucepan and bring to a boil. Cover and boil for 2 minutes, then remove from heat. Stir in the citrus peel and let steep for 1 hour. Transfer the zest and syrup to an airtight container and store in the refrigerator until needed.

EQUIPMENT

The following kitchen appliances and utensils will make creating the desserts in this book easy and enjoyable.

- A blender or large-capacity food processor is called for in almost all of the recipes. A 4-cup blender with variable speed settings is the first choice for puréeing fruit; a single-speed blender will take slightly longer to purée the ingredients completely. A food processor, fitted with a metal blade, may also be used, but make sure it will hold at least 5 cups of liquid. If you do not have a large-capacity food processor, purée the fruit in batches.

- Citrus juices are used in varying amounts in the vast majority of these recipes. While a hand juicer will do the job, an electric juicer will extract more juice from each piece of fruit and save your wrist for whisking zabaglione. A stainless-steel juicer that rests on its own fitted bowl provides stability when pressing fruit and will hold up to 1 cup of juice. Many food processors have juicer attachments, and inexpensive free-standing units are widely available. Electric juicers will extract the most juice from each piece of fruit.

- Many recipes call for grated citrus zest. Use the small rasps of a grater or a zester.

- A large metal bowl, a double boiler, and heavy-duty baking sheets are also called for throughout this book. These are essential items for a well-equipped kitchen and are worth the investment.

- There are essentially three types of ice cream makers on the market: hand-cranked machines, motorized machines, and machines with compressors. Hand-cranked and motorized machines require you to freeze a cylinder for at least 6 hours before preparing a sorbet or ice cream. Machines with compressors require little or no prefreezing, allowing for more spontaneous preparation.

Hand-cranked machines require vigilance and can take up to 40 minutes to freeze ingredients. The Donvier is the best-known and most widely available machine. It has a well-insulated cylinder and a clear top for easy viewing. The components of the Donvier can be separated for easy cleaning and storage.

Motorized machines have the advantage of not requiring constant attention. Once the prepared ingredients are poured into the pre-frozen cylinder, you can leave them running for 20 to 40 minutes, the average range of time it will take to freeze a sorbet or ice cream. With their built-in motors, these machines take up slightly more storage and counter space than a hand-cranked machine. Krups and Maverick make competitively priced, widely available machines.

Sunbeam Oster makes a motorized machine that does not require prefreezing a cylinder. Instead, a brine of salt and ice is prepared and poured around a blender-shaped container. While the machine churns, additional ice and salt are added through openings at the corners of the container. A plastic cover is provided so that the completed dessert does not need to be transferred to another container for storage.

Machines with compressors are the Cadillacs of ice cream machines. Their built-in compressors quickly freeze the cylinder, providing a frozen dessert in less time. These same compressors make these machines heavy and bulky. The newly introduced Williams-Sonoma machine takes up a third of the counter space of the Simac, a machine that has been on the market a longer time. Both machines have removable cylinders for easy cleanup. The Williams-Sonoma stainless-steel cylinder comes with a lid so that it may be placed directly in the freezer until you are ready to serve. Another attraction of the Williams-Sonoma machine is a secondary built-in cylinder that enables you to make another batch of sorbet or ice cream immediately after the first batch is done. These machines are substantially more expensive than either the hand-cranked or motorized machines. But if you make sorbets and ice creams regularly, they are your best choice.

INGREDIENT SOURCES

Duane Park Cafe is located in TriBeCa, a neighborhood in lower Manhattan renowned for its restaurants. TriBeCa—which comprises the Triangle Below Canal Street—has a long history as a center for fine food. From before the Civil War until 1968 the area was home to New York City's most important food market, Washington Market. While largely replaced by residential lofts, some food purveyors still maintain wholesale and retail operations in TriBeCa. Chefs Seiji Maeda and John Dudek rely on some of these suppliers for the special ingredients included in their recipes. They are listed here along with other distributors of fine foods and ingredients.

A. L. Bazzini Company, Inc.
339 Greenwich Street
New York, NY 10013
800-228-0172

Bazzini has been located in TriBeCa since 1886. They offer a holiday catalogue featuring a wide variety of whole and ground nuts. Their retail store will ship items year-round.

Diamond Organics
P.O. Box 2159
Freedom, CA 95019
800-922-2396
Fax: 800-290-3683

Organically grown fruits and vegetables are the specialty of Diamond Organics. Peaches, apples, Moro and Sansuinelli blood oranges, and a wide variety of dried fruits and nuts of the highest quality are offered in their catalogue.

Freida's
P.O. Box 58488
Los Angeles, CA 90058
800-241-1771

Freida's products are widely available in grocery stores. Dried fruits, unsweetened coconut flakes, and nuts can also be ordered directly from either their extensive catalogue or their product list, which are provided on request.

Indian River Groves
P.O. Box 3689
Seminole, FL 33775
800-940-3344
Fax: 813-397-3049

An excellent source for all types of fresh citrus, including ruby red grapefruit, navel oranges, tangerines, and the exceptionally sweet and juicy honeybell oranges. Indian River Groves also mails select pears and apples. Call for their free catalogue.

Polarica
73 Hudson Street
New York, NY 10013
212-406-0400

Polarica is a gourmet food purveyor offering an extensive selection of game, poultry, pâtés, berries, and mushrooms to restaurants all over the world. It is an excellent source for fresh and frozen fruits as well as fruit purées. Their list includes black currant, mango, and blood orange purées. There is a minimum order requirement on all products; however, all fruits are shipped frozen in several small trays. Use just the amount called for in the recipe and keep the rest frozen for another time.

Walnut Acres
Penn's Creek, PA 17862
800-433-3998
Fax: 717-837-1146

The Walnut Acres catalogue features a wide variety of organic dried fruits, flours, fresh produce, and syrups.

Williams-Sonoma
P.O. Box 7456
San Francisco, CA 94120-7456
800-541-2233
Fax: 415-421-5153

Williams-Sonoma's national chain of kitchen supply stores are a good source for D'Arbo black currant syrups (and others), which are imported from Austria. It is also an excellent source for cookware, pure extracts, ground chocolate, and other specialty foods.

Harry Wils & Co., Inc.
182 Duane Street
New York, NY 10013
212-431-9731

Harry Wils began its illustrious career in TriBeCa selling butter and eggs in 1921. Today, proprietor Steven Wils offers an extensive list of products including nuts, fruit purées (blood orange, mango, coconut, blackberry—to name a few), frozen fruits (whole strawberries, black-berries, blueberries), and imported baking chocolate to local customers. New Yorkers can contact Wils to purchase these quality products directly. They do not currently ship their products.

BIOGRAPHIES

Located at 157 Duane Street in Manhattan's TriBeCa neighborhood, Duane Park Cafe combines the warmth of a neighborhood bistro with a spare and elegant Asian influence. The inviting facade beckons patrons inside, where they are warmly greeted by general manager Alfred A. Chiodo. They pass the well-stocked bar with its colorful rattan-topped stools and enter the serene dining room. The softly lit room is always accented with a spectacular flower arrangement created by chef and owner Seiji Maeda. The promise of excellent food is soon deliciously fulfilled in this charming restaurant.

Born and raised in Japan, **Seiji Maeda** moved to New York in the 1970s. He graduated from the Culinary Institute of America in 1981. His postgraduate work took him from the Cajun kitchen of K-Paul's in New Orleans to the French cuisine served at Hubert's and the renowned Regine's, both in New York City. In January 1989, Maeda opened Duane Park Cafe. He combines the influences from western cuisines with his own background to create dishes that defy ethnic categories.

John Dudek has been the pastry chef at Duane Park Cafe since 1990. Originally trained as a painter, he came to New York to study nutrition at the Pratt Institute in Brooklyn. John joined the kitchen at Hubert's, where he worked for ten years, the last seven as pastry chef. His recipes have been featured in various magazines and newspapers, including *Food & Wine, Gourmet, The New York Times, New York Magazine,* and *Newsday.*

Joy Simmen Hamburger and Mimi Shanley Taft are coauthors of *The TriBeCa Cookbook: Menus from New York's Most Renowned Restaurant Neighborhood* (Ten Speed Press, 1995).

INDEX